Kids
PARTY
Cakes

KÖNEMANN

Helpful Hints For Successful Cake Decorating

Cake making and decorating should be fun. Here are some hints to help make cake decorating enjoyable and successful without intricate designs or the use of a template.

Creepy Bat, page 28

◆ Assemble all the ingredients and utensils before you start baking or decorating the cake.
◆ Use the correct sized and shaped tins. We take our measurements across the top of tins.
◆ Prepare tins before you begin. Brush tin/s with melted butter or oil. Line base and side/s with paper; grease the paper.
◆ Preheat oven to moderate 180°C.
◆ Establish size of board to be used, allowing ample space around the cake. Masonite is ideal for a cake board.
◆ Boards can be covered with foil, foil-covered paper, cellophane or wrapping paper of your choice.

◆ To cover a round board, cut a circle 5 cm larger than the board. Spread smooth surface of board with children's glue and press into centre of wrong side of paper. Cut extension at 2 cm intervals around board. Fold paper over edge of board and secure to back of board with tape. Cut a round of paper and glue over back of board.
◆ To cover a rectangular or square board, cut paper 5 cm larger than the board. Spread smooth surface of board with children's glue and press into centre of wrong side of paper. Fold corners, press firmly towards back of board and secure with tape. Cut a rectangle or square of paper and glue over back of board.
◆ Bake cakes for suggested cooking time or until a skewer comes out clean when inserted into centre of cake.

Basic Butttercake
150 g butter
3/4 cup caster sugar
3 eggs
1 teaspoon imitation vanilla essence
1²/3 cups self-raising flour
1/3 cup milk

WARNING Always remove skewers from cakes before you serve them. Never use toothpicks to hold cakes together. They can easily be hidden in a serving and a child can choke on them.

1 Preheat oven to moderate 190°C. Brush tin (see chart, opposite, for sizes) with melted butter or oil. Line base and side with paper; grease paper.
2 Using electric beaters, beat butter and sugar in small mixing bowl until light and creamy. Add eggs gradually, beating thoroughly after each addition. Add essence; beat until combined.
3 Using a metal spoon, fold in sifted flour alternately with milk. Stir until just combined and mixture is almost smooth. Be careful not to overmix.
4 Spoon mixture into prepared tin; smooth surface. Bake 35 minutes or until a skewer comes out clean when it is inserted in centre of cake.
5 Leave cake in tin 5 minutes before turning onto wire rack to cool.
Buttercakes can be baked up to 3 months before using. Cover with plastic wrap and store in freezer. Remove from freezer, stand, uncovered, 10 minutes before cutting to shape. Stand further 15 minutes before decorating. Freeze leftover cake pieces and use later for desserts if desired.

Fluffy Icing
1¼ cups caster sugar
½ cup water
3 egg whites
1 Combine sugar and water in small pan. Stir constantly over low heat until mixture boils and sugar has dissolved. Simmer, uncovered, without stirring 5 minutes.
2 Using electric beaters, beat egg whites in a clean, dry mixing bowl until stiff peaks form.
3 Pour hot syrup in a thin stream over egg whites, beating constantly until icing is thick, glossy and increased in volume.

Basic Buttercream
125 g butter
1⅓ cups icing sugar, sifted
1 tablespoon milk
1 teaspoon water

1 Beat butter in small mixing bowl until light and creamy.
2 Gradually add sugar, milk and water, beating for 5 minutes or until mixture is smooth, light and creamy.

You will need 1 x 340 g packet cake mix or 1 quantity basic buttercake to fill the following sized tins used in this book	
17/20/23 cm	deep round cake tin
15/19/23 cm	deep square cake tin
20 cm	ring tin
30 x 20 cm	shallow oblong cake tin
21 x 14 x 7 cm	deep bread/loaf tin
25 x 15 x 5.5 cm	shallow bread/loaf tin
2 – 26 x 8 x 4.5 cm	long bar tins
30 x 25 x 2 cm	shallow Swiss roll tin
5-cup capacity	pudding steamer
5 x 1-cup capacity	timbale tins
30 x 25 x 2 cm	shallow Swiss roll tin
The following sized tins require 2 x 340 g packets or 2 quantities basic buttercake recipe:	
28/30 cm	deep, round cake tin
7-cup capacity	pudding steamer
9-cup capacity	pudding steamer
10-cup capacity	dolly vardin tin

Drum

1 covered board
2 x 20 cm purchased
   sponge cakes
1/4 cup strawberry jam
2 quantities buttercream
green food colour
1.5 metres green ribbon
large piping bag
no. 2 piping nozzle
liquorice allsorts
coloured cachous
2 chopsticks

1 Sandwich sponge
cakes together with
jam. Position on board.
2 Tint half the icing
pale green. Divide
remaining icing into
two portions. Leave one
portion plain, tint
second portion dark
green. Spread plain
icing over top of drum;
pale green icing around
side of drum.
3 Cut ribbon into

required lengths to fit
around side of drum.
Press ribbon onto side
of cake in zig-zag
pattern.
4 Using sharp knife, cut
liquorice allsorts into
evenly-sized slices. Press
onto side of cake. Pipe
dark green icing over
top rim of drum. Cover
chopsticks with foil and
place sweets on end to
make drumsticks.
Complete cake as
illustrated.

HINT
When tinting icing,
remember that a little
food colouring goes a
long way and that the
colour will darken
when it is left to
stand. Start with only
a drop or two of
colouring, mix well
and add more drops
as needed.

1. Spread strawberry jam over sponge
and place second sponge on top.

2. Spread plain icing over the top of
drum, pale green icing around sides.

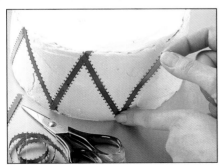

3. Cut green ribbon into lengths and arrange in zig-zag pattern around drum.

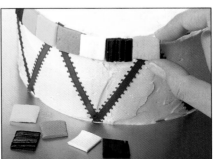

4. Arrange liquorice allsort slices around sides of drum.

Teddy Bear

1 covered board
9-cup capacity pudding
    basin cake
5-cup capacity pudding
    basin cake
2 x 300 g purchased
    sponge rolls
2 purchased jam
    rollettes
2 flat chocolate biscuits
1 quantity fluffy icing
caramel food colour
liquorice strips
assorted sweets
35 cm ribbon

1 Cut 3 cm off one end
of large cake and 1 cm
off opposite end. Stand
on prepared board on
3 cm cut edge.
2 Cut 1 cm across
smaller cake. Attach
head to body with
skewers. Cut a 3 cm
slice off each sponge
roll; discard. Attach
sponge rolls and jam
rollettes onto cake with
skewers. Tint all but
1 cup icing with
caramel colour.
3 Spread caramel icing
over all of cake. Attach
ears to head with
skewers. Using a fork,
spread plain icing onto
belly, head and paws
as shown.
4 Decorate cake as
illustrated. Attach
ribbon last.

1. Cut a slice off both
ends of pudding basin cake.

2. Assemble cake with
skewers.

3. Swirl plain icing onto
belly, head and paws.

4. Decorate cake with
biscuits, sweets and bow.

HINT

We've chosen to make this teddy bear in the
traditional teddy bear colour. But he could just as
easily be iced with blue or red or green, or stripes
or polka dots. Cake decorating is a form of
self-expression - so express yourself!
There's no reason for teddy to be a male. A girl
teddy could be iced in pink, with a deeper pink
bow, and perhaps given some yellow popcorn
for her hair.

Happy Humpty on the Wall

1 covered board
20 cm purchased
  sponge cake
25 x 15 x 5.5 cm loaf
  cake
2 quantities
  buttercream
egg-yellow and caramel
  food colours
2 x 250 g packets
  oblong chocolate
  biscuits
assorted sweets
50 cm coloured ribbon

1 Using a sharp knife, trim edges of sponge to form an egg shape.
2 Position cut Humpty shape onto loaf cake (wall), using skewers. Divide icing into two equal portions. Tint one portion egg-yellow and the other portion caramel.
3 Spread front, back, top and sides of wall smoothly with caramel icing. Press chocolate biscuits onto wall in brick pattern as shown, cutting them to fit. Spread all over Humpty's head with yellow icing.
4 Decorate Humpty's face with assorted sweets as illustrated. Position big ribbon bow onto Humpty's neck last.

1. Cut sponge into large oval shape for Humpty.

2. Attach oval to loaf cake with skewers.

3. Press chocolate biscuits into wall in brick pattern.

4. Make face with sweets and finish with bow.

HINT

This is one of the easiest cakes to make, ideal for a first-time cake decorator. Children can help with the decorating, too, for their own party or for a younger brother or sister.

Make sure the buttercream is at room temperature before you ice the cake. If it is too cold, it will be hard to spread, and rough handling could cause the cake to crumble into pieces.

Clown

1 covered board
deep, 23 cm round cake
5-cup pudding basin
 cake
1 large muffin
250 g packet jam
 rollettes
2 quantities
 buttercream
pink, black, blue,
 yellow, violet and
 green food colours
2 small piping bags
2 plastic eyes
liquorice twists
toasted marshmallow
assorted sweets

1 Place round cake
onto prepared board.
Turn pudding cake on
its side; cut 1 cm off
one end of cake.
Attach, cut-side down,
onto round cake with
skewers.
2 Cut 1 cm slice
diagonally off one side
of head; hat will be
placed here. Cut
rollettes in half. Divide
icing into three
portions. Tint all but
1 tablespoon of one
portion deep pink; tint
remaining tablespoon
dark grey. Tint
two-thirds of second
portion pale pink; make
remaining one-third
blue. Divide third
portion of icing into

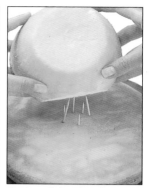

1. Attach head with
skewers.

3. Pipe smiling mouth on
clown in deep pink icing.

three portions; tint
yellow, violet and green.
Spread base with
two-thirds deep pink
icing; spread pale pink
over head. Cover top
and sides of rollettes
with coloured icings;
arrange on cake as
shown in photograph.
3 Pipe mouth onto

2. Cover top and sides of
rollettes with icing.

4. Place muffin in position
for hat; decorate face.

cake with reserved deep
pink and overpipe a
smiling line in dark grey.
4 Spread muffin (hat)
with blue icing; attach
hat to side of head
with skewers or
icing. Position eyes
onto face. To complete
cake, decorate as
illustrated.

Alphabet Blocks

1 covered board
2 x deep, 23 cm square
  cakes
2 quantities
  buttercream
pink, yellow, green,
  apricot and violet
  food colours
large piping bag
no. 9 fluted piping
  nozzle
coloured sweets

1 Sandwich both cakes
together with
buttercream. Trim
edges; cut cake into
four squares.
2 Divide icing into six
portions. Tint two
portions pink and each
of the four remaining
portions a different
colour. Spread a
different colour icing
over each side of blocks.
3 Pipe a shell border

along edge of each side
of the blocks with one
portion of pink icing.
4 Carefully arrange
onto prepared board as
shown. Complete cake
as illustrated.

HINT
These blocks may be
decorated any way
that appeals to you.
You can pipe faces
onto them, or people,
objects or animals;
you can make
abstract designs with
icing or sweets; you
can put numbers on
them; or your
children can make up
their own patterns.
It's important to
arrange the blocks
before you do your
final decorations,
because if they're
moved, you could
ruin your design.

1. Sandwich cakes with buttercream and
cut into four.

2. Spread a different-coloured icing on
each side of blocks.

3. Pipe a shell border in pink icing around all the edges.

4. Arrange cakes and form letters with coloured sweets.

1. *Spread sandwiched cake with icing and cover with sprinkles.*

2. *Pipe lines to indicate frills and fill in with coloured icing.*

Jack-in-the-box

1 covered board
2 x deep, 23 cm square
  cakes
20 cm purchased
  sponge cake
2 quantities buttercream
coloured sprinkles
blue, violet, orange,
  yellow and red food
  colours
large piping bag
small piping bag
5 mm plain piping
  tube
liquorice strap
assorted sweets
marshmallows

1 Sandwich square
cakes together with
buttercream. Place on
prepared board. Divide
icing into two portions.
Spread one portion
plain icing over square
cake; reserve ⅔ cup for
face. Press sprinkles

over top and sides of
cake using a large
palette knife.
2 Divide remaining
icing into four portions.
Tint each one a
different colour (not
including red). Pipe
lines with plain icing
onto one sponge to
mark frills. Spread
colours alternately onto
frill within the lines,
as shown.
3 Position frill onto
sprinkle-covered cake.
Cut liquorice into
strips. Arrange on frill
as shown, with
marshmallows.
4 Position head onto
frill using skewers. Tint
reserved plain icing
yellow. Spread over
head. Tint 2 teaspoons
leftover yellow icing
red for the lips.
Pipe lips onto face as
shown. Complete cake
as illustrated.

3. Arrange liquorice strips and marshmallows on frill.

4. Place Jack's head on frill, ice and decorate as shown.

15

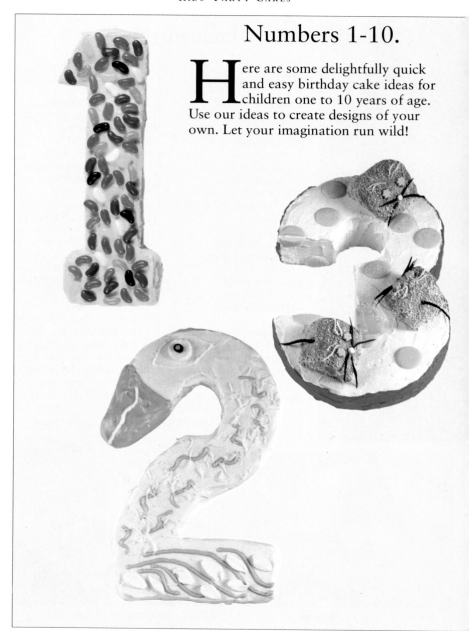

Numbers 1-10.

Here are some delightfully quick and easy birthday cake ideas for children one to 10 years of age. Use our ideas to create designs of your own. Let your imagination run wild!

1 covered board
2 – 26 x 8 x 4.5 cm
   long bar cakes
1 quantity buttercream
egg-yellow food colour
jelly beans

1 Place one bar cake onto board. Cut second bar cake in half crossways. Use one half as base of number one.
2 Cut diagonally across corner of remaining piece for the top of the number. Assemble cake as shown.
3 Tint buttercream yellow and spread over cake.
4 Press jelly beans all over top of cake as illustrated.

1 covered board
26 x 8 x 4.5 cm
   long bar cake
20 cm ring cake
3 jam rollettes
1 quantity fluffy
   icing
pink food colour
6 white
   marshmallows
1 liquorice allsort

1 Cut a quarter off bar cake. Use long piece for base of number two. Reserve small piece.
2 Cut out one-fifth of the ring cake. Assemble cake pieces on board as shown. To make beak, place 2 rollettes in position at top of number two and place the third one on top of them in the centre, pyramid-style.
3 Tint 2/3 cup icing dark pink, all but 2 tablespoons pale pink.
4 Decorate cake as illustrated.

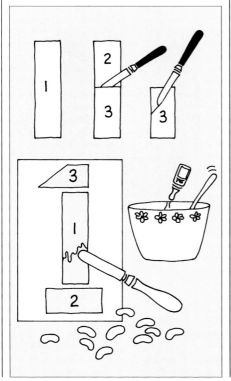

1 covered board
2 x 20 cm ring cakes
1 quantity
 buttercream
red and black
 food colours
assorted sweets
liquorice
desiccated and
 shredded coconut

1 Cut out one-quarter of first ring
cake; set aside. Place remainder on
board as base of number three. Cut
out one-third of second cake; shape to
fit against base. Assemble as shown.
2 Cut three half circles from leftover
cake pieces for mice.
3 Divide icing in two. Leave one
portion plain. Tint all but ½ cup of
remaining icing red; tint remaining
icing grey.
4 Decorate as illustrated.

1 covered board
3 – 26 x 8 x 4.5 cm
 long bar cakes
1 quantity fluffy
 icing
blue food colour
silver cachous
tiny posy of flowers
ribbon

1 Place one bar cake onto board. Cut
one-quarter off second bar cake, set
aside. Cut diagonally across each end
of remaining bar cake.
2 Assemble cake as shown.
3 Tint icing soft blue. Spread over
top and sides of cake.
4 Press cachous all over cake and
decorate with flowers and ribbon.

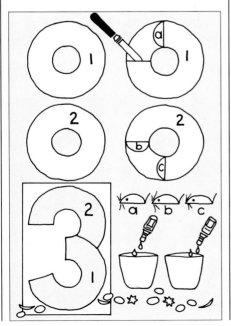

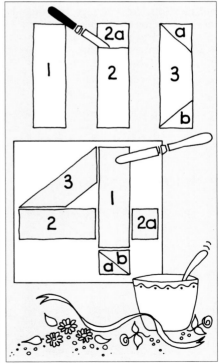

20 cm ring cake
1 quantity
   buttercream
egg-yellow food
   colour
250 g packet
   oblong
   chocolate
   biscuits
   liquorice strap
1 covered board
26 x 8 x 4.5 cm
   long bar cake
1 piping bag
no. 2 plain
   piping nozzle

1 Cut one-third off bar cake. Cut out a quarter of ring cake. Assemble cake on board as shown.
2 Reserve 2 tablespoons plain icing. Tint remaining icing yellow.
3 Cover cake with yellow buttercream. Press enough biscuits on top of cake for dominoes. Use plain buttercream to pipe dots on dominoes.
4 Cut liquorice into strips. Position onto cake as illustrated.

1 covered board
20 cm ring cake
300 g jam roll

1 quantity
   buttercream
twisted licorice
   cut into 1 cm-
   wide pieces
liquorice allsorts
green and violet
   food colours
no. 2 plain
   piping nozzle
2 paper piping
   bags

1 Place ring cake right-side up on board. Cut jam roll 2 cm diagonally across one end and 4 cm diagonally across the other. The larger end will be used for head.
2 Assemble cake as shown. Position head, cut-side down, on ring cake.
3 Tint all but ½ cup buttercream bright green. Tint 2 teaspoons icing violet, and remaining icing pale green.
4 Spread top and sides of cake with bright green icing. Use pale green to pipe scales on snake; violet for brows. Decorate cake as illustrated.

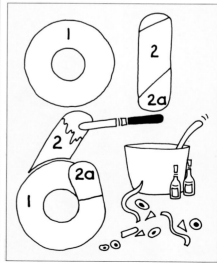

1 covered board
2 – 26 x 8 x 4.5 cm
    long bar cakes
1 quantity
    buttercream
caramel and orange
    food colours
no.12 fluted piping
    nozzle
2 piping bags
assorted sweets
liquorice strap

1 Place one bar cake onto board for top of number seven and cut a small curve into top left side. Round off end for nose and cut another shallow curve on right-hand side of cake.
2 Cut second bar cake 1 cm diagonally across both ends. Position one of cut-out pieces on top of second cake as shown. Assemble cakes.
3 Tint all but 1 cup buttercream caramel-brown; spread over cake. Tint reserved icing orange. Pipe blotches as shown. Tint leftover icing dark orange. Use to outline blotches.
4 Cut liquorice into pieces for mane. Decorate as illustrated.

1 covered board
2 x 20 cm ring cakes
2 quantities
    buttercream
blue food colour
liquorice straps
1 plastic train set

1 Cut 2 cm off base of both ring cakes. Assemble cakes as shown.
2 Tint buttercream blue, spread over top and sides of cake.
3 Cut liquorice into thin strips. Position long strips on cake for railway line, making it the same width as train set. Place short strips across tracks.
4 Complete cake as shown.

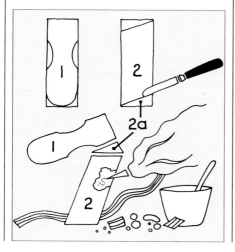

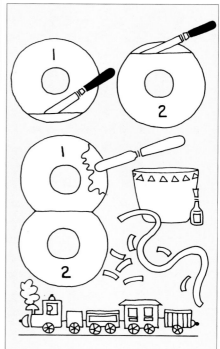

2 quantities
  buttercream
blue and orange
  food colours
paper piping bag
no. 2 plain
  piping nozzle
1/3 cup spearmint
  leaves
4 marshmallows
2 tablespoons
  yellow sprinkles
assorted sweets

1 covered board
20 cm ring cake
26 x 8 x 4.5 cm
  long bar cake

1 Place ring cake onto board. Cut
4 cm diagonally across one end of bar
cake. Curve slightly to fit against ring
cake. Tint ½ cup icing orange;
remaining icing blue.
2 Spread top and sides of cake with
blue buttercream.
3 Pipe orange petals onto cake, fill
with orange icing as shown.
4 Cut marshmallows in half. Pinch
ends to shape. Top with sprinkles.
Complete cake as illustrated.

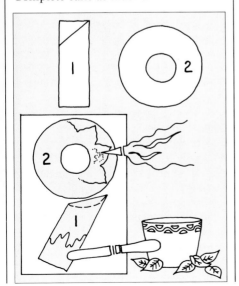

20 cm ring cake
2 cupcakes
2 quantities
  buttercream
red and black
  food colours
piping bag
no. 2 plain
  piping nozzle
10 flat mints
silver cachous
50 cm red
  curling ribbon

1 covered board
2 – 26 x 8 x
  4.5 cm long
  bar cakes

1 Place one bar cake on its side, on
board. Place a cupcake at each end as
mouthpiece for receiver. Cut second
bar cake in half. Freeze one half for
later use.
2 Cut remaining half in two. Cut ring
cake in half. Assemble cakes on board
as shown.
3 Tint all but 3 tablespoons icing red.
Tint remaining icing black. Spread
top and sides of cakes with red icing.
4 Pipe black numbers onto mints.
Decorate cakes as illustrated.

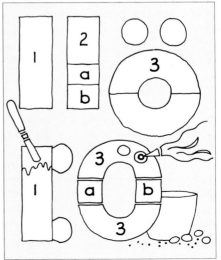

Pirate Pete

1 covered board
30 x 20 cm oblong cake
20 cm purchased
  sponge cake
2 quantities buttercream
violet, caramel and
  chocolate-brown food
  colours
1 small paper piping bag
1 large paper piping bag
no. 22 fluted piping
  nozzle
20 toothpicks
flat chocolate-coated
  biscuit
silver cachous
liquorice strips
assorted sweets

1 Cut oblong cake into
shape of hat as shown.
2 Position hat on
board. Reserve 1/3 cup
plain icing. Divide
remaining icing into
three portions. Tint one
portion dark violet,

second portion caramel
and third portion
chocolate-brown.
Spread violet over hat.
3 Position head onto
hat. Spread caramel
icing over face. Use
large bag with nozzle
and brown icing to pipe
pirate's hair.
4 Tape toothpicks
together firmly. Dip
ends into brown
colouring and dab onto
pirate's chin as shown.
Pipe skull and
crossbones and right
eye with plain icing in
small bag. Complete
cake as illustrated.

HINT
Add colouring to
icing gradually. Use
the tip of a skewer to
tint small amounts of
icing; an eye dropper
can be used for
larger quantities.

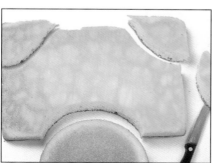

1. Cut pieces out of oblong cake to form
hat shape.

2. Place hat on prepared board and cover
with violet icing.

3. Position face on board, ice and pipe on brown icing for hair.

4. Decorate face. Use toothpicks to dab on whiskers.

Miss Dolly Vardin

1 covered board
1 x 10-cup dolly vardin
  cake
2 quantities buttercream
pink and lemon-yellow
  food colours
silver and pink cachous
15 cm doll
40 cm lace trimming
12 pink ribbon roses
no. 5 and no. 20 piping
  nozzles
3 small paper piping
  bags

1 Trim cake surface.
Centre on prepared
board and attach with a
little buttercream. Press
doll firmly but carefully
into cake to waist
level. Tint one-third
icing lemon-yellow.
Tint 1/3 cup icing soft
pink; tint remaining
icing deep pink.
2 Mark underskirt
scallops onto cake with
a skewer. Pipe
lemon-yellow icing with
no. 20 nozzle onto
cake, starting at base.
Make rows of scallops.
3 Swirl deep pink icing
onto remaining cake
and use no. 5 nozzle to
pipe deep pink on
bodice and soft pink
trim on dress.
4 Decorate cake as
illustrated. Position lace
onto dress last.

1. Press doll firmly into
cake up to waist.

2. Pipe underskirt scallops
onto base.

3. Swirl pink icing onto
remaining cake.

4. Place lace around
bottom of dress last.

HINT

To make a small paper piping bag, you will need a
sheet of greaseproof paper 30 x 30 cm, and
30 x 40 cm for a large bag. Fold in half
lengthways. Hold folded edge in left hand, fold
and twist paper with right hand to form a cone.
Tape or staple along outside of cone. Spoon icing
into bag; press towards tip. Fold ends over bag
to enclose icing; snip tip off bag. Use a slow and
steady squeeze to pipe icing onto cake.

Creepy Bat

1 covered board
deep, 28 cm round cake
6 cm round cutter
1 quantity fluffy icing
black food colour
small piping bag
no. 2 piping nozzle
assorted sweets

1 Cut cake in half. Cut
three half circles along
straight edge of each
cake half using the
cutter to form scallops.
2 Arrange the bat
wings onto prepared
board. Join 2 half
circles together for bat
body as shown. Tint all
but 1 cup icing dark
grey. Tint remaining
icing black. Spread grey
icing over top of wings
and bat body. Give the
icing on the wings a
rough texture with a
fork. Spread all but 2

tablespoons black icing
below wings.
3 Pipe black icing
around body and wings
as shown.
4 Insert skewers into
sweets for ears and
attach to head. Decorate
cake as illustrated.
Stick-on stars and
moons may be placed
on the board if desired.

HINT
Trim top and sides of
cakes with a serrated
knife for best results.
Use underside of
cake as top; it will
produce a smoother,
flatter surface.
Fully-iced cakes can
be made ahead and
frozen for up to
three months.
Decorate with
sweets and ribbons,
etc, on the day to
be used.

1. Using cutter, cut three half circles from
straight edge of each cake half.

2. Place pieces on board, cover top of
wings and body with dark grey icing.

3. Pipe black icing to outline bat body and wings.

4. Decorate face as shown. Use skewers to attach sweets as ears.

Robby Robot

1 covered board
21 x 14 x 7 cm loaf cake
300 g purchased sponge
    roll
2 quantities buttercream
red, green, orange and
    violet food colours
4 lollipops
2 chocolate antennae
assorted sweets
2 small piping bags
no. 2 piping nozzle

1 Stand loaf cake
upright on prepared
board, right-side facing
the front. Trim base if
necessary. Cut a 3 cm-
wide slice from sponge
roll; cut in half to form
feet. Position at base of
robot as shown.
2 Cut a 6 cm-wide slice
from roll for head.
Divide icing into two
portions. Tint one
portion red. Leave ½
cup untinted. Tint 3
tablespoons green, 1
tablespoon orange and
remaining icing violet.
Spread red icing on
body and violet on feet.
Spread a rectangle in
centre of body with
plain icing for control
panel. Spread head with
plain icing; attach it to
the body with skewers
or icing.
3 Pipe orange lines and
mouth using a piping

1. Position sponge roll
slices at base for feet.

2. Ice parts. Attach head
to body with skewers.

3. Use bag with nozzle for
details on body.

4. Press lollipops into
sides for arms.

bag without a nozzle.
Pipe green lines, dots on
feet and squiggles
around face using a bag
fitted with nozzle.
4 Press two lollipops
into sides of cake for
arms; attach antennae
to head. Decorate
remaining cake as
illustrated.

HINT
Spread a small
quantity of icing onto
the prepared board
and place cake on it.
This will prevent the
cake from sliding
around when it is
being decorated,
transported or stored.

Spinning Spaceship

1 covered board
deep, 30 cm round cake
1 quantity fluffy icing
lemon-yellow, egg-
  yellow, red and black
  food colours
1 liquorice strap
3 small paper piping
  bags
2 chocolate-coated
  marshmallow biscuits
silver cachous
4 lollipops
assorted sweets

1 Cut an 8 cm-wide slice across the cake and cut slice in half.
2 Place halves onto prepared board, on either side of the remaining cake (ship body) as shown.
3 Tint ¼ cup icing red and ¼ cup icing black. Reserve 1 tablespoon plain icing. Divide remaining icing into two portions. Tint one portion lemon-yellow, remaining portion egg-yellow. Spread lemon-yellow icing over main body of spaceship; egg-yellow over base.
4 Use red and black icings to pipe windows and lines as shown. Cut liquorice into 3 mm-wide thickness. Place onto spaceship as shown. Position spacemen and lollipops as shown. Pipe on face with plain icing. Complete decorating cake as illustrated.

HINT
Piping bags are sometimes needed for the finishing touches. Use a paper piping bag and discard when finished or use a cloth or plastic bag.

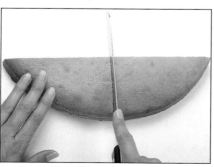

1. Cut a slice off bottom of cake, and cut it in half.

2. Position pieces on either side of remaining cake.

3. Use lemon-yellow icing for top half of cake; egg-yellow for base.

4. Pipe on details; position spacemen, sweets and lollipops.

Sam Snowman

1 covered board
12 cm cardboard circle
9-cup pudding basin
  cake
5-cup pudding basin
  cake
1 large purchased
  cupcake or muffin
1 quantity fluffy icing
black food colour
coloured cachous
assorted sweets
twisted liquorice stick
toothpicks
rubber band
50 cm ribbon

1. Cut out ring from cardboard circle.

2. Cover head and body with plain icing.

3. For hat, place muffin on ring and ice black.

4. Make broom of toothpicks and liquorice.

1 Cut a 4 cm circle from centre of 12 cm cardboard circle to form a ring. Place large cake onto prepared board. Stand small cake on its side, cut 2 cm across cake. Position small cake to fit onto larger cake using skewers or icing to attach.
2 Tint 1 cup icing black; leave remaining icing plain. Spread plain icing roughly over snowman.
3 Spread black icing onto one side of cardboard ring and muffin. Position ring onto snowman's head. Attach muffin to cake with skewers through centre of ring to make hat.
4 Decorate hat with cachous and add finishing touches as illustrated. Place ribbon around snowman's neck and tie loosely. Do this last. To make broom, attach toothpicks to liquorice stick with rubber band.

HINT
Flat-bladed knives, palette knives, rubber or plastic spatulas are ideal for spreading icing onto cakes. Forks can be used for swirling or creating lines or special effects on the icing.

1. Trim sides off bar cake for peaked roof; place on top of trimmed loaf cake.

2. Add slices of honey roll to each end of loaf cake; colour ark and roof as shown.

Noah's Ark

1 covered board
25 x 15 x 5.5 cm
  shallow loaf cake
26 x 8 x 4.5 cm long
  bar cake
300 g purchased honey
  roll
2 quantities buttercream
orange, pink and violet
  food colours
2 x 200 g packets
  chocolate-coated
  liquorice logs
200 g packet wafer
  biscuits
2 x 15g milk chocolates
assorted sweets
animals

1 Cut corners off loaf cake; arrange on prepared board. Cut lengthways across top of bar cake to create a peaked roof for the cabin. Place along centre of loaf cake.

2 Cut two 5 cm-thick slices from honey roll. Position one at each end of trimmed loaf cake. Divide icing into three portions. Tint one portion orange, one portion pink and one portion violet. Spread orange over sides of ark. Spread pink on deck and violet over cabin as shown.

3 Press wafer biscuits onto both sides of the cabin roof.

4 Arrange chocolate liquorice logs around base of ark. Complete cake as shown.

HINT
Jam rollettes, Swiss rolls, lemon or honey rolls, muffins, cupcakes and assorted biscuits and sweets are readily available in supermarkets.

3. Stick wafer biscuits on both sides of shaped roof.

4. Cover sides with liquorice logs; decorate with animals and sweets.

Wilma Witch

1 covered board
30 x 20 cm shallow
  oblong cake
deep, 23 cm square cake
1 quantity fluffy icing
orange, violet, green
  and blue food colours
2 small paper piping
  bags
currants and raisin
liquorice twists and
  strips
assorted sweets

1. Trim oblong cake for hat, square cake for head.

2. Place cakes in position on board.

1 Cut out hat from oblong cake and witch head from square cake as shown.
2 Arrange cakes on prepared board. Tint half icing orange, 3 tablespoons icing violet for lips, 1 tablespoon green for veins in eye; remaining icing blue for hat.
3 Using a palette knife, spread blue icing over hat; orange over face.
4 Pipe lips onto cake. Using appropriate sweets, place teeth and eye onto cake; pipe veins on eye. Use currants for warts on chin and raisin for mole on nose. Arrange liquorice for hair, and make insects on hat out of sweets. Decorate with remaining sweets as illustrated.

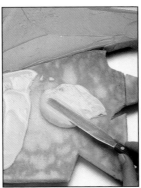

3. Use blue icing for hat, orange for face.

4. Pipe lips. Add eye, teeth and hair. Decorate.

HINT
You may need a piping nozzle for some cakes. These are available at department stores and kichenware shops.
If you are using a piping nozzle, cut 1 cm off the end of bag before filling it with icing. Insert nozzle, then spoon icing into bag.
Coloured icing will darken on standing; always start by tinting it a shade lighter than you think you will need.

Lovable Lucy

1 covered board
20 cm purchased round
  sponge cake
30 x 20 cm oblong cake
2 purchased jam
  rollettes
2 x 4-cm wide slices,
  purchased jam roll
2 quantities buttercream
pink and green food
  colours
2 cups coloured popcorn
2 toasted marshmallows
assorted sweets
pink cachous
20 cm lace trim
plastic eyes
2 bows

1 Place sponge at top of prepared board. Shape oblong cake into dress as shown. Position onto board with head, arms and feet as shown.
2 Reserve ½ cup plain icing for feet. Tint 1 cup icing pink for face; tint remaining icing green for dress. Spread pink over face and arms, green over dress and plain icing over feet.
3 Press popcorn onto head for hair.
4 Use marshmallows at ends of arms for hands. Decorate cake as shown, finishing with lace trim on dress and ribbon bows on feet.

1. Cut oblong cake to shape; assemble all pieces.

2. Spread coloured icings over head and body.

3. Use coloured popcorn on round cake for hair.

4. Decorate feet with ribbon bows.

HINT

Always place cake into position on your prepared board before you start to decorate. If you decorate a cake, then try to move it you can undo all your good work. If you're worried about drips as you go, choose foil or foil-covered paper to cover the board – spills can easily be wiped off. In hot weather, refrigerate an iced cake if it has to stand for any length of time before the party, otherwise chocolates and sweets may melt.

Cool Cat

1 *covered board*
deep, 30 cm round cake
1 *quantity fluffy icing*
pink, caramel and black
  food colours
2 *small piping bags*
liquorice strips
2 *large white*
  marshmallow
black sweets

1 Cut cake into cat
face shape as shown.
Place cake in position
on prepared board.
2 Tint 2 tablespoons
icing pale pink,
2 tablespoons black and
½ cup icing dark
caramel. Tint all but
2 tablespoons of the
remaining icing pale
caramel. Mark cat's
facial features onto the
cake with a skewer and
pipe features onto cake
with the plain icing. Fill

mouth with pink.
3 Spread muzzle with
dark caramel icing,
nose with black.
Spread pale caramel
icing over remainder of
cake. Place pink
triangles in ears.
4 Outline muzzle and
features with black as
shown. Cut liquorice
strips and use for
eyebrows and whiskers;
use black sweets for
pupils of marshmallow
eyes. Complete cake
as illustrated.

HINT
Let your children help
decorate the cake if
they want to. The
finished cake may not
be as professional as
perhaps you would
like, but your children
will love it and be
proud of their
contribution.

1. Cut cake into shape, with ears and
whiskers, and place on board.

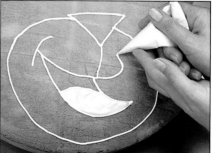

2. Mark out facial features and pipe with
plain icing. Fill mouth with pink.

3. *Ice muzzle with dark caramel, nose with black, rest of face with pale caramel.*

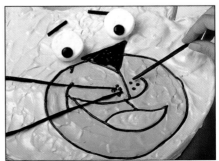

4. *Outline face with black, and decorate with liquorice strips and sweets.*

Perfect Parfait

1 *covered board*
30 x 20 *cm oblong cake*
4 *purchased cupcakes*
1 *quantity fluffy icing*
egg-yellow, violet,
  caramel and pink food
  colours
assorted sweets,
  hundreds and
  thousands

1 Cut oblong cake
into shape of tall
parfait glass. Place
onto prepared board.
Position cupcakes at
top of glass as shown,
cutting one of them into
pieces to make the top
look more like realistic
scoops of ice-cream.
2 Leave 1 cup icing
plain. Tint ⅓ cup icing
violet, ⅓ pink, ¼ cup
caramel and remainder
yellow. Spread caramel
over base of glass.
3 Spread coloured
icings onto cake as
shown. Swirl plain icing
over cupcakes.
4 Sprinkle cupcakes
with hundreds and
thousands. Decorate
the body of the glass
with sweets as
illustrated. We've
chosen sweets in the
same colours as the
icings, but you can use
contrasting colours if
you prefer.

1. *Cut cake into glass
shape; top with cupcakes.*

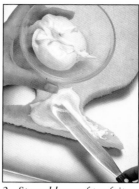

2. *Spread base of parfait
glass with caramel icing.*

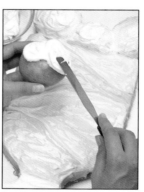

3. *Colour rest of glass and
cupcakes as shown.*

4. *Finish with sweets and
hundreds and thousands.*

HINT

Place desiccated or shredded coconut into a freezer
bag with 1 drop food colouring. Wearing thin
disposable gloves, rub colour into coconut with
fingertips to desired shade, adding colour as
necessary. You can get a very interesting effect by
using multi-coloured desiccated coconut.
To toast shredded coconut, spread on a tray and
grill or bake at medium heat, stirring regularly,
5 minutes or until golden.

1. Cut into sides and curve end of loaf cake to shape dog's body.

2. Place muffin, sponge roll pieces and jam rollettes in place.

Rusty the Dog

1 covered board
25 x 15 x 5.5 cm
  shallow loaf cake
1 large muffin
250 g sponge roll
4 purchased jam
  rollettes
2 quantities buttercream
caramel food colour
1/2 cup cocoa powder,
  sifted
liquorice strap
1 teaspoon shredded
  coconut
assorted sweets

1 Place loaf cake onto a board, right side up. Round ends of cake as shown. Cut a curve into each side of cake to shape dog's body.
2 Position on prepared board. Trim muffin for head to fit against body as shown. Cut 4 x 2 cm slices from sponge roll.

Attach a slice either side of cake for hind legs. Position jam rollettes onto board as shown for front legs and paws of hind legs. Cut remaining sponge slices in half. Position two halves towards front of dog for ears. Secure another half towards back of cake for tail.
3 Tint two-thirds icing caramel-brown. Leave 2 tablespoons icing plain. Combine remaining icing with cocoa; blend until smooth. Spread caramel icing over entire cake.
4 Place dark-brown icing onto back and top of head. Use a fork to spread the brown and plain icing to other parts of the body. Decorate as illustrated, using liquorice strap for collar and shredded coconut for whiskers.

3. Cover the whole cake with caramel-brown icing.

4. Spread brown and plain icing with fork. Decorate with liquorice and coconut.

Rabbit Surprise

1 covered board
30 x 20 cm oblong cake
deep, 23cm square cake
1 quantity fluffy icing
black and pink food
  colours
100 g packet pink
  marshmallows, cut in
  half
liquorice strips
assorted sweets
1 small paper piping bag

1 Cut oblong cake into
rabbit head as shown.
Cut square cake into
hat as shown. (Note
that rabbit is popping
out of upside-down
hat.) Assemble cakes on
board. Divide icing in
half. Tint one portion
black; ⅓ cup pale pink,
and remaining icing
pale grey.
2 Spread black icing
smoothly over hat.
Swirl grey icing over
rabbit head.
3 Pipe pink icing onto
rabbit for ears and
eyebrows as shown.
4 Press marshmallows
in straight rows onto
hat. Decorate rabbit
head with sweets as
illustrated, using
straight liquorice strips
for the whiskers, a pale
pink sweet for the nose
and a red jelly bean for
the mouth.

1. Shape oblong cake for head, square cake for hat.

2. Ice hat in black, rabbit head in pale grey.

3. Use pink icing for details on ears and face.

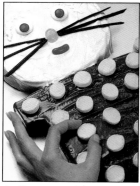

4. Decorate with marshmallows and sweets.

HINT
You'll find it's easiest to use a sharp knife to cut
sugar- and chocolate-coated sweets. Liquorice and
marshmallows, lace, braid and ribbon are best cut
with scissors.
Choosing sweets for decorating is great fun, and
tests your ingenuity. Popcorn makes good hair,
as do liquorice strips. Whites of eyes can be
made with marshmallows, adding little coloured
candy-coated chocolates for irises.

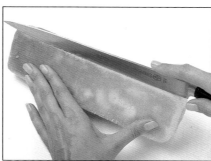

1. Cut bar cake diagonally across whole length to make pitched roof.

2. Spread base with green icing, house with apricot, and roof with lemon-yellow.

Candy Cottage

1 covered board
30 x 20 cm oblong cake
deep, 23 cm square cake
26 x 8 x 4.5 cm long
  bar cake
2 quantities
  buttercream
lemon-yellow, apricot,
  green and violet food
  colours
250 g after-dinner mints
liquorice strips
liquorice allsorts
musk sticks
hundreds and thousands
assorted sweets and
  biscuits

1   Place oblong cake onto prepared board. Cut square cake in half. Place one half on top of the other. Position across centre of oblong cake. Cut diagonally across length of bar cake. Position onto house as roof.

2   Divide icing into three portions. Reserve 1 tablespoon plain icing. Tint one portion lemon-yellow, one portion apricot and remainder green. Spread green icing over base, then apricot over house, followed by the lemon-yellow roof. Tint remaining lemon icing violet; use for curtains on wafer windows.

3   Cut mints in half diagonally. Position onto roof as shown.

4   Make steps with coloured musk sticks; arrange liquorice allsorts around the front and sides of the cottage. Spread a wafer biscuit with reserved plain icing and sprinkle with hundreds and thousands. This makes the front door. Don't forget the chimney.

3. Cover roof with tiles made of mints cut in half diagonally.

4. Trim with sweets for steps, fence and front door, and finally the chimney.

Choc-mint Dinosaur

1 covered board
2 x 23 cm round cakes
2 quantities
 buttercream
green and red food
 colours
small piping bag
1 cup milk chocolate
 melts, cut in half
100 g bag spearmint
 leaves
sweets for toes, eyes
 and brow

1 Cut one cake in half. Cut two half circles along flat side of each cake half as shown.
2 Cut second cake as shown in photograph.
3 Assemble cake on prepared board, but do not attach head. Tint all but ⅓ cup icing green. Tint 3 teaspoons icing red; leave rest plain.
4 Spread green icing over entire cake. Attach head to body using skewers; ice head. Use a fork to spread plain icing randomly over body. Pipe red mouth onto cake. Cut spearmint leaves down the centre and arrange along dinosaur's head and back. Press chocolate melts over body at an angle. Complete cake with sweets as illustrated.

> ## HINT
> Snakes make perfect mouths, or you can buy lolly lips; a red jelly bean is an effective small mouth. Black whiskers can be made from liquorice strips, white whiskers from shredded coconut. Finely cut liquorice makes good eyelashes and brows.

1. *Cut one cake in half, then cut out half-circles with cutter.*

2. *Cut second cake as shown. This will form the centre body of the dinosaur.*

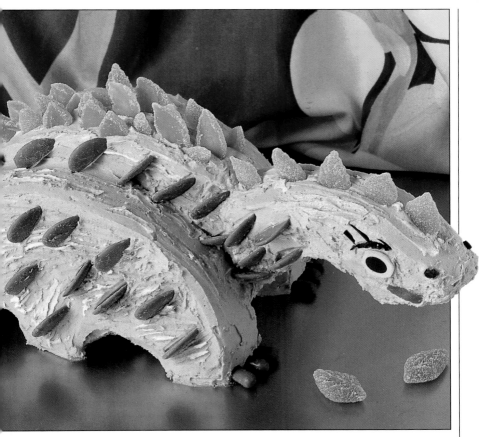

3. Assemble cake; ice body before
attaching head with skewers then ice head.

4. Spread plain icing at random over
body. Finish dinosaur as shown.

Mr Mouse

1 covered board
deep, 30 cm round
  cake
2 quantities
  buttercream
black, red and yellow
  food colours
2 small piping bags
no. 2 plain piping
  nozzle
¾ cup chocolate
  sprinkles
6 large chocolate
  biscuits
1 large prune
1 large pink
  marshmallow
sweets for eyes

1. Cut cake as shown; use cut-out piece for chin.

2. Ice face yellow; outline hair, cover with sprinkles.

1 Carefully cut into one side of cake to form nose as shown. Place leftover cake under face to form Mr Mouse's rounded chin. Assemble the cake in position on prepared board.
2 Tint ¼ cup icing black, ⅓ cup icing red, and make the remaining icing yellow. With a palette knife, spread yellow icing smoothly over entire face. Use a skewer to outline hair area. Fill area liberally with chocolate sprinkles as shown.
3 Pipe outline of mouth onto cake with red icing, then fill in the

3. Pipe and fill mouth. Outline features in black.

area with red icing. Position three chocolate biscuits on each side of head for each ear. Use black icing to outline eyes, brows and lashes, as well as nose.
4 Position prune on tip of the nose, fill in eyes with sweets, place marshmallow on cheek.

4. Add eyes, biscuits for ears and prune for nose.

HINT
To make a cake of your child's favourite cartoon character, trace and then simplify it, keeping its identifying features. Use the colours associated with the character.

Casey Caterpillar

1 covered board
2 x 250 g packets jam
  rollettes
1 large purchased
  cupcake or
  muffin
1 quantity fluffy icing
apricot and green food
  colours
jelly beans
assorted sweets
plastic eyes
sugar lips
coloured popcorn
20 cm coloured ribbon

1 Arrange jam rollettes on prepared board in a wavy pattern for caterpillar body, and place cupcake at front for head. Tint all but ¼ cup icing apricot; tint reserved icing green.
2 Spread apricot icing over ends, top and sides of line of rollettes and over side of cupcake. Spread top of cupcake with green icing.
3 Press brightly coloured sweets at random onto top, and pairs of jelly beans at intervals along sides of caterpillar as feet.
4 Attach eyes and lips to face and pile popcorn onto head. Tie ribbon into bow, attach.

HINT
For a busy mother, this is a particularly easy party cake to prepare, since it uses only purchased cakes – there is no cooking involved. The only thing you'll have to make is the icing. Casey Caterpillar can be assembled very quickly and could easily be made by even young children.

1. Arrange rollettes in wavy pattern on board for body, with cupcake for head.

2. Cover ends, top and sides of body and side of head with plain icing.

3. *Press sweets randomly over caterpillar body; ice top of head green.*

4. *Place eyes and lips in position; add popcorn hair, and finally the bow.*

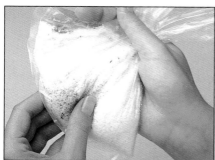

1. *Place coconut and green food colour in plastic bag and press between fingers.*

2. *Place cakes side-by-side on board and cover with green icing.*

Soccer Field

1 covered board
2 – 30 x 20 cm oblong
  cakes
1 quantity buttercream
green food colour
1/2 cup desiccated
  coconut
small piping bag
no. 2 piping nozzle
plastic soccer team with
  goal posts

1 Place cakes side-by-side on board. Place coconut in plastic bag with 2 drops food colour. Press between fingers to mix. Tint all but 1/4 cup icing pale green.
2 Ice cake green.
3 Place a 30 x 20 cm tin across centre of field. Sprinkle coconut around. Remove tin.
4 Pipe field lines with plain icing. Press goal posts and men in place.

3. Sprinkle coloured coconut around edges of the field.

4. Pipe lines onto cake as shown, and position men and goal posts.

Noughts-and-crosses

1 covered board
2 – 30 x 25 x 2 cm
  shallow Swiss roll
  cakes, not rolled
1 quantity buttercream
pink and violet food
  colours
liquorice strips
250 g packet iced
  biscuits
musk sticks
coloured sugar-coated
  chocolates
small piping bag

1 Place Swiss roll cakes on top of each other. Tint all of icing except for 1 tablespoon deep pink. Tint the reserved icing violet. Spread pink icing smoothly over top of the cake.
2 Cut liquorice into long thin strips; press onto cake to make squares as shown.

3 Press sugar-coated chocolates into squares as noughts and use musk sticks to make the crosses.
4 Spread icing on back of biscuits and press around the sides of cake. Use bag and violet icing to pipe in corner 'you win' or 'happy birthday', or whatever is appropriate.

HINT
Other board games you could make are draughts, with biscuits as counters, snakes-and-ladders, using snake lollies and liquorice strips for the snakes and ladders, backgammon, Chinese checkers or chess (with plastic chess pieces – or as close as you can get to them with sweets).

1. Position Swiss roll cakes on top of each other, spread top with pink icing.

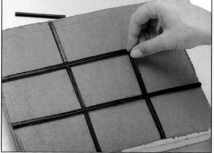

2. Press long thin strips of liquorice onto cake to form squares.

3. Make noughts and crosses by pressing sweets onto cake.

4. Press biscuits around sides of cake as the finishing touch.

Kimberley Kite

1 covered board
2 – 30 x 20 cm oblong
  cakes
1 quantity fluffy icing
red food colour
hundreds and thousands
small piping bag
coloured popcorn
2 chocolate biscuits
assorted sweets
1 m curling ribbon
250 g hundreds and
  thousands biscuits

1 Arrange cakes side-by-side on a cutting surface. Cut cakes into shape of kite as shown. Cut leftover cake into 6 x 7 cm triangles. Position the kite and triangles onto the prepared board.
2 Tint ¼ cup icing red; leave remainder plain. Spread plain icing over top and sides of kite and triangles.
3 Sprinkle tops of triangles with hundreds and thousands.
4 Pipe mouth onto cake with red icing as shown. Decorate cake as illustrated with popcorn for hair, biscuits and sweets for eyes, brows and nose, and curling ribbon for kite string. Finally, press biscuits firmly around sides of kite.

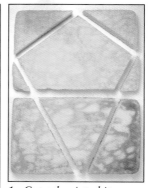

1. Cut cakes into kite shape as shown.

2. Cover kite shape and triangles with white icing.

3. Sprinkle triangles with hundreds and thousands.

4. Pipe on mouth, add other facial features.

HINT

It's a lovely idea to make a cake that reflects your child's interests. You could make a cricket bat and ball, a football, a dart board, a book, a paintbox. More ambitious decorators could try their hand at a camera, a telephone or a computer. You could even try to make a portrait of your child, or show him or her engaged in some favourite activity. It doesn't have to be perfect – just be sure you get the eye and hair colours right.

Index